REMEMBERING
Hannah

A JOURNEY THROUGH LOSS WITH HOPE

GARY AND MARI MALYCHEWSKI with
SHIRLEY QUIRING MOZENA

ISBN (paperback): 979-8-9891355-7-8
ISBN (ebook): 979-8-9891355-8-5

Library of Congress Control Number: 2025918467

Cover design: Kara Starcher of Mountain Creek Books LLC

Jesus said, "Let the little children come to me,
and do not hinder them,
for the kingdom of heaven belongs to such as these."
Matthew 19:14, NIV

Table of Contents

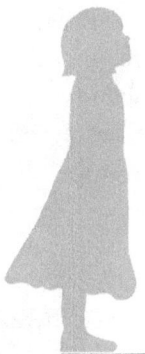

Preface

My life is but a weaving
Between my God and me.
I cannot choose the colors
He weaveth steadily.
He knows, He loves, He cares;
Nothing this truth can dim.
He gives the very best to those
Who leave the choice to Him.

~ The Weaver 1892 (Grant Colfax Tullar, 1869–1950)

"We just want to make sure we've taken all the steps we should,"
Gary said as our GriefShare group told their stories.
His wife, Mari (pronounced Mare-ee), nodded in agreement.

My husband Jim and I facilitate a grief class twice yearly, working with people who've lost a loved one in death. It was January 2024, and Gary and Mari had experienced one of the most difficult losses in life, though on the outside they looked no different than any ordinary couple—raising their family, living ordinary lives. Yet underneath, theirs was a story of endurance and sorrow. They had walked through the destructive storm of loss.

There we sat around a large conference table, the faint scent of coffee lingering as each person clutched a workbook with suggestions and questions, reading aloud and discussing Bible passages about grieving and God's presence in our pain.

The group was a mix of men and women grieving their losses. One woman, Sue, was grieving the loss of her best friend. Another, a Gen-Xer, her mother. One grieved her grandmother, whom she called "granny." One had lost a father. Another, a baby boomer, her husband.

These are typical losses, but in this group, there were five parents grieving the loss of a child. Three of them had each lost an adult son. But Gary and Mari had lost a little girl—only seven years old.

It seems natural for an older person to die—for we all die. But when a child is taken in death, the difficulties seem harder. When our parent or sibling dies, our past shimmers away. They're no longer there to answer questions about what came before. When our spouse dies, we've lost the present and the past with that person. But our child. We've lost our future. We had hoped that child's name and story would be passed on to future generations, but that life has been snuffed out. And a child of only seven years? An incomparable loss.

At this afternoon's session, we'd read from the poet, Solomon, in the Bible:

> *There is a time for everything,*
> *and a season for every activity under the heavens:*
> *a time to be born and a time to die. . . .*
> *a time to weep and a time to laugh,*
> *a time to mourn and a time to dance.*
> (Ecclesiastes 3:1-2, 4)

"Was it really time for Hannah to die when she was only seven?" Hannah's mother asked.

"It is very hard to understand why God would allow the accident that took Hannah's life. I didn't understand it either when my daughter died in her sleep when she was only thirty-one years old with a little boy to raise," Jim said.

"I think God gave me a warning about six months before the accident," Gary said after I read the poem aloud. "I almost hit a girl on my route the summer before Hannah died." He continued to tell the story about how he might have so easily killed a little girl.

After he finished the story, I asked him then and there if I could have his and Mari's permission to include Hannah's story in an article I was writing about forgiveness.

A few weeks later, the couple met with my husband and me. We discussed

writing a story about their little Hannah, but as we talked, we realized the story needed to be a book. Their journey, marked by Hannah's enduring grace, became this book to share their story of loss and faith with others. You will learn who Gary and Mari are. Their past. Their time of nearly indescribable sorrow. How they learned to carry on after that heartbreaking loss.

It is my hope you will be encouraged and strengthened by their story, whether you are in a storm of loss and grief right now or when that storm comes. And it will.

This is their story.

Chapter 1

Just an Ordinary Cloudy Day in December

We strive to provide service excellence for those communities that place their trust in our company and are always dedicated to putting our customers first.
~ Waste Connections, Solid Waste Industry

Six lives were forever changed on a gray December morning in 1997, in a quiet Vancouver, Washington, neighborhood near the mighty Columbia River. Nearly thirty years later, in the spring of 2025, I interviewed these six in several sessions, their memories as sharp as the chill in the Pacific Northwest air.

The morning of that fateful day dawned overcast, heavy clouds draping the sky like a woolen blanket. No rain fell, but the mist hung thick, leaving a cool dampness on the skin. Traffic hummed softly through the fog, a muted soundtrack to a typical winter day in the Pacific Northwest.

Mari, thirty-one, was a stay-at-home mom, homeschooling her two oldest. Hannah was seven and soon to turn eight, her bright eyes sparkling with curiosity. Caleb was anticipating his sixth birthday that Saturday. Josiah, three, toddled around, his small feet pattering on the hardwood floors. That morning, their home in west Vancouver felt warm against the outside chill, the aroma of oatmeal simmering on the stove and faint sunlight struggling through the curtains.

Gary, thirty-two, drove for UPS during the chaotic Christmas season. He started early, the rumble of his truck engine vibrating through his seat as he loaded parcels, the cold air sharp in his lungs. His route wound through rural

communities west of Portland, Oregon, each delivery a step in the holiday rush.

Kris Wright, a twenty-three-year-old driver for Waste Connections, began his route in the older west side of Vancouver, Washington. The neighborhood's modest homes lined rain-slicked streets. Bare trees extended their stark branches against the gray sky. The chill of the steering wheel seeped through Kris's gloves as he navigated his clunky, lever-operated truck, the bitter taste of his morning coffee lingering. Waste Connections, a scrappy $15 million outfit in 1997, had just acquired the industry's largest player, setting their sights on a public offering that would fuel an almost $10 billion future by 2025. For Kris, though, the job was about the rhythm of the alleys—gravel crunching under tires, bins clattering into the hopper, and the occasional smile from a kid like the little girl on "I" Street who brought him a tin of cookies on holidays.

Ron Mittelstaedt, CEO of Waste Connections, was on a business trip, striding through an airport jetway. The metallic clang of footsteps echoed around him, mingling with the faint whiff of jet fuel. His cell phone buzzed in his pocket, insistent. It was Darrell Chambliss, his Executive Vice President of Operations, calling from Vancouver, Washington. Ron's company, formed earlier that year with about 250 employees, was a fledgling force in the solid waste industry, hungry for growth.

Darrell had started his day at the company's newly acquired disposal plant in a rural stretch outside Vancouver, where he was overseeing the transition from the previous owners. The plant thrummed with the low growl of machinery, the sharp scent of waste and diesel cutting through the crisp morning breeze. Darrell answered his phone's insistent ring. "There's been an accident," the dispatcher said.

Neal Curtiss was the pastor of Vancouver Community Church, his role a divine calling that anchored his life. He lived in a cozy home near the church with his large family, their laughter a constant warmth. After a busy weekend of sermons and community events, followed by a restful Monday off, Tuesday marked his return to the office. The scent of freshly brewed tea filled the air, the soft click of his computer keyboard a familiar rhythm. But his plans— perhaps reviewing notes or preparing for evening services—would shatter when his phone rang, vibrating on the wooden desk, with the frantic voice of Mari Malychewski on the line.

Each of these people—Mari with her kids, Gary on his travels with

deliveries, Kris on his route, Darrell at the plant, Ron on his travels, Neal at church—had their own story, unfolding in the misty embrace of Vancouver. None could have known what this ordinary cloudy day held, a moment that would bind their lives forever.

Chapter 2

The Beginning

A child who is raised in a difficult environment
learns to adapt and survive in that environment,
often developing a resilience that can serve them well in later life.
~ Anonymous

On a cool September evening in 1985, Gary Malychewski (pronounced Mal-chess-kee) and Mari Comstock met at the Lighthouse, a Christian coffee house on Main Street in Vancouver, Washington, their eyes glowing under the twinkling glow of string lights. The air carried the rich scent of roasted coffee and the faint sweetness of cinnamon rolls from the counter, while the soft strum of a guitar filled the room. Both new Christians, they were brimming with the joy of their faith in Jesus Christ.

"Hey, I'm Gary," he said, extending a hand, his brown eyes crinkling with a friendly smile. "You new here?"

Mari, her cheeks flushed from the crisp outside, nodded. "I'm Mari." She laughed, her voice light but nervous, tucking a strand of blonde hair behind her ear.

Mari and Gary remained friends for the next few years, chatting over coffee, the clink of mugs punctuating their talks. They both dated other people. Mari volunteered at the Lighthouse every Friday night. The group of volunteers met for prayer at 7:00 P.M., then went out at eight to invite young people to come in.

One Friday evening in December 1987, her roommate suggested they go to the coffee house. "It'll be fun, Mari," she said, grinning. "Plus, there might be cute guys." Mari had been in a serious relationship that had ended the summer of 1987. Her heart was raw.

Gary was there again. They lingered long after the coffee house closed, their conversation spilling into the cool evening as they stood under a flickering streetlamp. This time, something shifted.

"Would you like to go to the Josh McDowell event next week?" Gary asked.

"Sure," she said.

That was the beginning of a change that would unfold in time.

Just friends, Gary & Mari

Chapter 3

Friendship Turns to Romance

Happy is the man who finds a true friend,
and far happier is he who finds that true friend in his wife.
~ Franz Schubert

On a cold December evening in 1987, Gary and Mari stepped into a bustling auditorium in Portland, Oregon, for a Josh McDowell event. The air buzzed with youthful chatter, the faint scent of popcorn drifting from the lobby as a cool draft slipped through open doors. McDowell's voice boomed through the speakers, his "Why Wait?" talk urging purity before marriage. As they left, streetlights cast a golden glow on the drizzle-glazed pavement.

Gary glanced at Mari, his hand brushing hers. "What did you think of that?" he asked, his breath visible in the chilly air as they walked to a nearby diner.

Mari's cheeks flushed, still warm from the auditorium. "It hit home, you know? I want to honor God in our relationship—if we keep going." She smiled, feeling a spark.

They settled into a booth, steaming hot chocolate warming their hands.

"What about you? What's your story, Gary? Why'd you nod so hard when McDowell talked about forgiveness?"

Gary took a sip, the sweet cocoa soothing his throat. "Guess I relate to needing a fresh start. Growing up wasn't easy. Born in '65, one of eight kids. We moved all over the Pacific Northwest—Astoria, Rainier, little towns by the Columbia River—chasing my dad's painting jobs. His alcoholism made home

tense. I'd hear beer bottles clinking, smell paint thinner everywhere. It was like walking on eggshells, waiting for his temper to flare."

Mari's eyes softened. "That sounds heavy. How'd you cope?"

"Nature," Gary said, his voice low. "I'd escape to the woods, feel the crunch of fir needles under my feet, smell the moss. Caught crawdads in creeks, the water so cold it numbed my fingers. Dad, when he was sober, took me fishing. Once, by a lake, he pointed at the sunset—fiery orange—and said, 'God made that, Gary.' That stuck with me, made me believe in a Creator."

Mari nodded, stirring her cocoa. "I get needing an escape. I was born in '66 in New York, but we moved to California, then up the Oregon coast near Reedsport. We were poor. I knew we were different, and my parents struggled to pay the mortgage and buy decent food. My mom and stepdad split when I was seventeen. I never knew my bio dad. And . . . there was abuse." Her voice wavered. "A family member, Duane, threatened me with a board that had nails poking out. Said he'd beat me if I told anyone."

Gary's jaw tightened. "Mari, that's awful. How'd you get through it?"

"At fourteen, I found my voice," she said, her eyes distant. "I told him, 'You're hurting me, Duane. I'm telling someone.' It didn't stop completely but slowed down. Later, at a family gathering, an uncle tried touching me. I snapped, 'Keep your hands off me!' He backed off. But I carried guilt, wondering if I could've stopped it sooner."

Gary reached for her hand. "You were brave. That took guts."

They sipped their drinks, sharing verses from their Bibles. Gary referenced Psalm 103:12, his voice soft: "As far as the east is from the west, that's how far God removes our sins. I've leaned on that. My past . . . it's not perfect either."

Mari tilted her head. "What do you mean?"

"When I was twelve, my brother Gerald—twenty, a genius at the University of Washington—took his life. Shot himself upstairs. I heard the crack, then this . . . heavy silence. He'd built a computer from an old TV, always laughing. But something ate at him." Gary's voice broke. "Dad drank more after that. Whiskey stench everywhere. For seven years, we couldn't say Gerald's name. At night, I'd hear Dad wail, 'Gerald, Gerald.' I'd lie on the grass outside, staring at the stars, asking, 'Is he with God?'"

Mari squeezed his hand. "I'm so sorry, Gary. That's a weight no kid should carry. . . ."

Their bond deepened over shared pain.

After an easy silence, Mari drew in a slow breath. "When I was young, I always felt used. Dirty. But in Longview, I worked for a Christian couple at a thrift store that smelled of old books and lavender. Their friendship changed me. They told me, 'God loves you, Mari. He died for you.' So when I prayed in '84, I felt forgiven. Clean. That's when I knew I could start over."

Gary nodded. "Same for me. At eighteen, I realized God wasn't just a Creator but someone who cared. Accepting Jesus changed me. God put people in my life to help me grow closer to him. Pastor Dan McNutt mentored me and even visited my brother, Paul, when he was in jail, offering hope. And Pastor Ralph Isensee, the pastor at First Baptist, preached directly from the Bible. I learned so much from them both. That's why I want us to start right."

One evening by the Columbia River, waves lapping and the earthy scent of mud in the air, Mari opened up more. "I want our family to be safe, loving," she whispered, trembling.

Gary pulled her close, his embrace warm. "Me too. We'll build that together."

Friendship had turned to romance. On a spring walk in a Vancouver park, cherry blossoms scented the air, petals soft underfoot. Gary kissed Mari, tender and gentle. "You make me feel safe," she said, heart racing.

"Safe enough to keep up with a macho baseball guy?" he teased, grinning.

She laughed. "You're not that macho."

In April 1988, in Gary's car outside Mari's apartment, as the sun dipped behind the hills, he turned to her. "Mari, will you marry me? I want to build a life with you, following God every step."

Tears filled her eyes. "Yes, Gary. You're the man I've always wanted. You're strong, you're handsome, but even better, you love God."

They chose a ring together and planned their wedding seven months away.

Gary's last baseball season with the University of Portland Pilots ended that spring, the crack of bats echoing. At home, the smell of paint thinner lingering, his father Emil confronted him. "Why quit, son? Scholarship, maybe pro ball," he said, disappointed.

"My heart's not in it, Dad," Gary replied firmly. "I want to get married, finish school, care for my family. That's my dream."

Their simple wedding took place on November 23, 1988, after the

Thanksgiving Eve service at First Baptist Church in Vancouver. Gary's mom sewed Mari's gown, smooth and elegant. Bridesmaids wore royal blue, groomsmen tuxedos with fuchsia accents for Gary's long-tailed tux. Mari's blonde hair swept under her veil, scent of lilies in her bouquet.

In the sanctuary, they vowed: "To have and to hold, for better, for worse, for richer, for poorer, in sickness and in health, to love and cherish, till death do us part." Gary's voice was steady, Mari's joyful.

As they left the church, Gary teased, "Honeymoon at my buddy's house, right?"

Mari swatted him, laughing. "You're kidding!"

They stayed at the Columbia Gorge Hotel, enchanted by its polished wood floors and crackling fireplace. Their commitment to purity made their first night in Room 342 magical. They returned regularly to the same room—when they could afford it—except for one anniversary in 1997.

They rented a one-bedroom apartment on Grand Avenue, near Mari's job at Jantzen Knitting Mill. Gary juggled working part-time as a sorter in the hub for UPS, held another job, and attended his classes. Their home was filled with laughter and shared meals.

In spring 1989, Mari turned to Gary one evening, her hands trembling slightly as she held a pregnancy test. The faint hum of rain tapped against the window, and the aroma of a simmering pot of stew filled the air.

"Gary, I'm pregnant," she said, her voice a mix of excitement and nerves, her eyes searching his.

He blinked, his ceramic mug clinking softly on the table. "You're sure?" he asked, a grin tugging at his lips.

"Very sure," Mari replied, laughing as she handed him the test, the plastic cool in his hand. They embraced, the wool of Gary's sweater soft against her cheek, their hearts racing with anticipation.

Engaged!

Wedding

Chapter 4

And Baby Makes Three

Daughters are far more precious than jewels.
~ Unknown

They moved into a larger apartment nearby, its wooden floors creaking underfoot, to prepare for their growing family. On January 11, 1990, a rain-mixed-with-snow day in Vancouver, Hannah Marguerite was born. In the hospital room, the sterile scent of antiseptic mingled with the sweet, honey-like fragrance of the newborn's skin.

Exhausted, Mari cuddled Hannah, marveling at her tiny fingers and toes, her soft downy head nestling perfectly in the palm of Mari's hand.

Gary leaned over, his breath warm, and whispered, "She's perfect, Mari."

That evening, as snowflakes swirled outside under the gray Pacific Northwest sky, Gary opened his Message Bible, the pages rustling softly. "Listen to this," he said, his voice steady with awe. "Psalm 139: 'Like an open book, you watched me grow from conception to birth; all the stages of my life were spread out before you, the days of my life all prepared before I'd even lived one day.'" They marveled, the words sinking in as they gazed at Hannah, her tiny chest rising and falling. God knew her before she was born, knew every day she would live.

They couldn't get enough of her. That first day, Hannah's lips curled into a smile—her trademark, a beacon of joy. "Look at that grin!" Gary chuckled, his finger brushing her soft cheek. A smiley, happy, contented baby, she grew into a joyful child, her laughter echoing through their apartment like a melody.

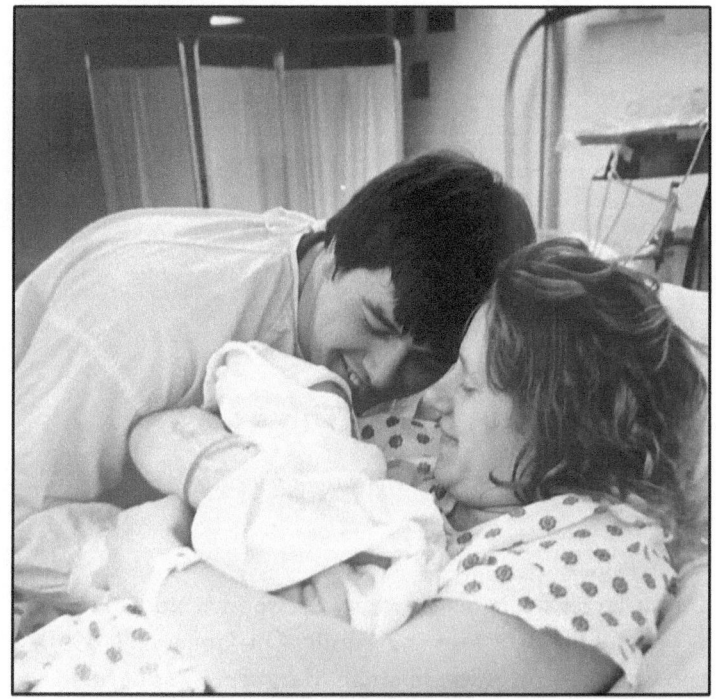

First look
at Hannah
Marguerite,
born January
11, 1990

Gary & Mari
with Hannah

After Hannah's birth, Mari quit her job at Jantzen Knitting Mill, the hum of sewing machines fading from her daily life. To supplement their income, she and Gary worked part-time as janitors at First Baptist Church, the faint scent of lemon polish lingering as they cleaned. Hannah, strapped in a backpack on Gary's back, gurgled happily, her tiny hands tugging at his hair as he vacuumed, the motor's drone mixing with her cooing.

On Hannah's first birthday, her brown eyes sparkled as they gathered in their apartment, the room bright with balloons and the sugary scent of a homemade chocolate cake. When Mari set the cake before Hannah, she plopped her face right into the frosting, eliciting peals of laughter. "That's our girl!" Mari exclaimed, wiping chocolate from Hannah's sandy-blonde curls. As the first grandchild on both sides, Hannah—feisty, stubborn, and full of smiles—was adored.

Hannah learned to love Jesus, just as her parents did. Mari sang hymns like "Jesus Loves Me" as she rocked her, the soft melody blending with the patter of rain outside. At three, Hannah prayed to receive Jesus, her small voice earnest as she said, "Jesus, come into my heart." Gary hugged her tightly, the warmth of his daughter's body a treasure.

Brown-eyed Hannah, with her sandy-blonde hair, had a knack for brightening days. Her friend Betsy once said, "Hannah's smile is the first thing you see—it lights up everything."

At the park, when a boy teased Betsy, Hannah stepped in, hands on hips. "Leave her alone!" she declared, her voice firm. She loved playing with Barbies, dressing them in tiny outfits, and she loved donning frilly dresses for dress-up, the fabric swishing as she twirled.

In August 1991, Gary earned his BS in business, diploma crisp in hand amid applause. "I wanted that degree," he'd told Mari, "so our kids have a better shot at college."

The family grew to four with Caleb's birth in late 1991. They found a house to rent and lived there until they'd saved enough money for a down payment. They bought their first home in 1994 on "I" Street in Vancouver, a dead-end street with no houses across the street, just open sky and the distant hum of Interstate 5 below. With their needing room for the kids to run and a safe street for biking, the place was perfect for their family.

Josiah was born in the spring of 1994, making their family a perfect size of five.

Family of five—Gary holding Caleb,
Mari holding Josiah, and Hannah in front

In their modest home, the family worked together. On sunny summer days, they planted a garden, the rich scent of soil and tomato vines filling the air.

"Pass me that trowel, Hannah," Gary called, sweat beading on his brow as he dug.

Weeding flower beds or tinkering in his garage shop, Gary taught the kids to help, their small hands tugging at weeds or holding tools, the metallic clank of a wrench punctuating their chatter.

Mari ensured the kids wore helmets when they rode their bikes, their laughter ringing as they pedaled on the quiet street, the breeze cool on their faces.

"Watch out, Caleb," Hannah instructed her brother when he veered toward another pathway.

"I'll take care of that, Hannah. I'm the mom here," Mari reminded her.

There were sometimes scraped knees to bandage and disagreements between siblings, but they were mostly a happy, contented family.

The community park, a few blocks away, was a favorite. Mari always went

Family on top of Beacon Rock (left to right)—Hannah,
Mari with Josiah in her pack, Gary holding Caleb

along, watching as the kids climbed slides and listening to the creak of swings
mixing with their giggles. "Stay where I can see you!" she'd call, her voice
carrying over the grassy field.

Now attending Vancouver Community Church, the family was active.
Hannah went to midweek Pioneer Club and Sunday School, the halls filled
with the chatter of kids.

Pastor Neal Curtiss, when asked about them, said, "Gary and Mari are a
close-knit family. Hannah's like a little mother to Caleb and Josiah—they look
up to her." He smiled, recalling her bossy yet loving ways.

Neighbors admired Gary and Mari's parenting. At a church picnic, a friend
watched Hannah share her sandwich with Josiah. "You two raise such kind
kids," she told Mari, who beamed, the taste of lemonade sharp on her tongue.
In their little home on "I" Street, with its worn carpets and cozy warmth,
they were content, their love and faith binding them amid the gentle rain of
Vancouver's winters.

Chapter 5

Model Parents

Children represent God's most generous gift to us.
~ Dr. James Dobson

In the cozy living room of their home on "I" Street, Mari bustled about, the faint scent of lavender from a candle mingling with the warm aroma of freshly baked bread cooling on the counter. It was a bright spring evening in 1997, and golden sunlight streamed through the windows, casting long shadows across the hardwood floor. Mari, ever the devoted mother, was teaching her boys to fold laundry, their small hands fumbling with socks. Hannah, now seven, sat nearby, her sandy-blonde hair catching the lamplight as she interpreted Josiah's garbled words for Mari.

Hannah with "her boys"

"Josiah says he wants the blue shirt," Hannah announced, her brown eyes bright with confidence.

Mari smiled, brushing a hand over Hannah's head. "You're such a good

big sister, Hannah. You understand him better than I do sometimes."

Hannah beamed. She was tough yet tender; Gary called her "Little Mari" for her resemblance to her mama, both in spirit and in care for "her boys."

Mari was an inspiration to other young mothers in their Vancouver neighborhood. At a community park playdate, the creak of swings and children's shouts filling the air, a neighbor, Ellen, watched as Hannah politely addressed her as "Mrs. Carter."

"I'm so impressed with your kids, Mari," Ellen said. "They're so obedient, calling adults 'Mr.' or 'Mrs.'—it's rare these days."

Mari laughed. "We just want them to respect others, you know? It starts at home."

Mari and Gary were committed to homeschooling their children, a growing but unconventional choice in the mid-1990s.

Over dinner one night, the clink of forks against plates punctuating their talk, Gary's sister voiced doubts. "Are you sure homeschooling's best?" she asked. "They need socialization, don't they?"

"We believe it's right for them," Mari replied firmly, her hand resting on Gary's. "We want to teach them our values—faith, respect, love—right here."

Gary nodded, his calloused hand squeezing hers, the warmth grounding their resolve. Living on his UPS driver's income meant sacrifices, but they were committed to Mari teaching at home.

Hannah adored her daddy, her hero. One sunny afternoon in their backyard, Gary stood beneath the garage's second-floor loft, arms outstretched. Caleb and Josiah had just jumped into his embrace, giggling wildly. Hannah, taller and heavier, hesitated, then grinned. "Catch me, Daddy!" she called, leaping without fear.

Gary caught her, his strong arms steady, the scent of sawdust from his workshop clinging to his shirt. "Always, Little Mari," he said, spinning her until she squealed.

Gary's UPS job meant late hours, the "beep" of his car's locking mechanism announcing his return home after dark. But homeschooling allowed flexibility; the kids started lessons later, which meant more evening time with Gary. "Who's ready for soccer?" he'd call, kicking off his boots and letting them thump on the floor.

Winter or not, Gary coached his "kiddos" with energy. On rainy evenings,

Hannah at the beach

when the Vancouver sky was too dark for outdoor play, he turned the living room into a soccer field, the front door one goal, the back door another. "Use your left foot, Caleb!" he instructed, the thud of a soft ball against the wall punctuating his words. "Make it as strong as your right!" All three kids were athletic, their skills honed by Gary's coaching. Hannah shone on the Westside Hounds soccer team, her hair bouncing as she darted across the field, damp grass sticking to her shins.

The family loved getaways, especially to Lincoln City, Oregon, eighty miles from Vancouver. Each January, they booked winter rates at a motel right on the beach, the salty ocean air and the crash of waves filling their senses.

One February evening in 1997, Gary burst through the door, his UPS uniform slightly rumpled, a grin spreading across his face. "Guess what?" he announced, the kids crowding around. "I won $500 in a work drawing!"

Mari's eyes widened. "That's enough for a trip to Lincoln City!" she said, clapping her hands.

"Can we go now?" Hannah asked, bouncing on her toes, the hardwood floor creaking.

"In May," Gary promised, ruffling her hair. "No school schedule holding us back."

In May, they packed their van and drove to Lincoln City. The Oregon coast greeted them with clear skies one day, the sun warm on their faces, and with gusty winds the next, requiring jackets. They lucked out with perfect beach days, the sand gritty underfoot as the kids built towering sandcastles, their laughter mingling with the squawk of seagulls. Hannah and Caleb dipped their toes in the icy Pacific, squealing at the cold, while Josiah tasted salt on his lips from the spray. Sunburned and tired, they returned home, the van filled with the scent of sunscreen and sandy towels.

Summer arrived, and the family planted a garden in their "I" Street backyard. Mari's spicy dilly beans—pickled green beans with dill weed and hot peppers—were a family favorite, the tangy crunch a staple at dinners. "Help me with these beans, Hannah," Mari called, accompanied by the clink of mason jars on the counter. Other days, they canned applesauce and peaches. Between tasks, the kids played, their bikes zipping down the quiet dead-end street, helmets snug under Mari's watchful eye.

One summer evening, as the sky glowed pink, Gary came home shaken, his face pale. Mari met him at the door. "What's wrong?" she asked, touching his arm, the fabric of his uniform damp from the day's work.

"Something happened on my route today," he said, his voice low, eyes distant. "I almost hit a girl near Vernonia."

Mari's breath caught, the air suddenly heavy. "Oh, Gary, are you okay?" she asked, guiding him to the couch.

He nodded slowly, the memory vivid. "I keep thinking . . . what if I hadn't stopped in time?" The kids, sensing the shift, gathered close, Hannah's small hand slipping into his, her touch a quiet comfort.

Chapter 6

A Timely Experience

When you follow God's will for your life, you can see how yesterday's events
prepared you for today's challenges and tomorrow's opportunities.
~ David Jeremiah

The kitchen glowed softly under a single overhead light, shadows dancing across the checkered linoleum floor. The faint sweetness of Mari's cinnamon apple pie hung in the air, blending with the earthy aroma of Gary's coffee. The family gathered around their scarred oak table, a testament to years of shared meals. Gary leaned forward, elbows on the wood, his hands cradling a chipped ceramic mug. Mari, her hair pulled back in a loose braid, revealing her high cheekbones and gentle expression, watched him with quiet intensity, her hazel eyes catching the light. Their three children waited for their father's story.

"Kids, Mari, you're not gonna believe what happened today," Gary began, his voice low but unsteady, still raw from the day's events. "I was driving through Vernonia, that little rural town with the old storefronts and quiet streets, finishing my route. It was late afternoon, the trees turning orange and red, the sky a clear blue with just a hint of gold. I had the radio on, listening to the crack of a baseball game—the Mariners were up by one in the seventh—when out of nowhere . . ."

He paused, his breath catching as the memory surged, vivid and fresh. The road through Vernonia had been calm, the only sound the hum of his truck tires on the worn pavement and the radio announcer's excited play-by-play.

Then, a blur—a small girl on a pink bicycle, streamers flapping, swerved into his lane from a side street.

"Bam!" Gary slapped the table, startling Caleb into dropping his fork. "There she was—a little girl, about Hannah's age. I swear, she appeared from thin air." In his mind's eye, Gary slammed the brake, and the van screeched and lurched slightly before stopping inches from the girl. His pulse thundered, and his hands gripped the wheel like a lifeline. "By some miracle—God's hand, I reckon—I stopped in time. I pulled over by the old post office and jumped out. My heart was pounding so hard I thought it'd burst."

He went back to that moment. Outside, the late afternoon air had been crisp, tinged with the scent of cedar and damp earth from the nearby woods, the sunlight casting long shadows across the street. Gary knelt beside the girl, his brown UPS uniform slightly wrinkled from a long day, his work boots sinking into the roadside dirt. Her bike wobbled as she stood frozen, clutching the handlebars.

"Hey, sweetheart," he said, forcing calm despite the tremor in his voice. "You okay? You scared me half to death. You gotta watch where you're going—I almost didn't see you."

The girl's blue eyes shimmered with tears, her lip trembling. She reminded Gary of Hannah at that age—same fearless spark, though with different hair—and his chest tightened.

He softened further. "I'm not mad, I promise. I've got a daughter your age—her name's Hannah. I'd lose my mind if something happened to her. Where's your home, kiddo? Let's get you back safe."

She pointed silently to a yellow house just down the street, its porch light glowing in the late afternoon haze. Roses climbed the white picket fence. Gary wheeled her bike as they walked along the cracked sidewalk, her small footsteps crunching beside him. At the door, he pressed the bell.

A tall man wearing a rumpled Oregon Ducks t-shirt answered. His face shifted from curiosity to alarm when he saw the girl. "Everything okay?" he asked in a tight voice.

"I'm Gary." Gary cleared his throat. "I almost hit your little girl with my UPS truck a minute ago. She darted out in front of me on her bike. Thank the Lord I stopped in time, but it was close."

The man's face drained of color. He dropped to one knee, pulling his

daughter close. "Emily, you okay, baby?" He looked up at Gary, eyes glistening. "Thank you. I don't know what I'd do if . . . " His voice trailed off.

Gary nodded, feeling the moment's weight. "I've got three kids—Hannah, she's seven, and my boys, Caleb and Josiah. If anything happened to them, it'd break me. Break us." He thought of Mari, and his throat tightened.

The father turned to Emily, his voice gentle but firm. "Em, promise me you'll look both ways. No more riding into the street like that. You're my world, you hear?"

Emily nodded, wiping her eyes. "I'm sorry, Daddy. I'll be careful."

"I'm Mark," he said as he offered Gary a handshake. Both men's eyes were wet, but their smiles eased the tension. "Why're we crying when she's standing right here?" Mark said, shaking his head.

Gary chuckled, wiping his sleeve across his face. "It's the what-ifs. They'll get you every time. Take care of her, Mark."

As Gary walked back to his van, the Vernonia sky was still bright with late afternoon light in the sleepy town. He slid into the driver's seat, the familiar creak of the seat grounding him, and whispered a prayer before driving home to Mari and the kids.

Back in the kitchen, Gary's voice grew quiet. "That moment's still with me, Mari," he said, meeting his wife's gaze. "Made me swear to drive slower, pay more attention. I kept seeing Hannah in that little girl—same age, same spark."

Mari reached for his hand, her touch warm and steady. "You were there for a reason, Gary. God's got a way of teaching us what matters."

Gary squeezed her hand, glancing at Hannah, who watched with wide, thoughtful eyes.

Chapter 7

An Anniversary Weekend to Remember

To get the full value of joy you must have someone to divide it with.

~ Mark Twain

The sage-green Craftsman Malychewski house was framed by towering evergreens. Its wide front porch was cluttered with potted mums and a weathered rocking chair, while the faint tinkle of a wind chime echoed from the eaves. Inside, the living room's worn hardwood floors creaked underfoot, bearing the scuffs and scratches of a family's life, and slants of late-afternoon light filtered through tall, double-hung windows. A faded quilt draped over the couch, Hannah's crayon sketches tacked to a bulletin board, and Caleb's baseball mitt tossed beside Josiah's toy trucks created a lived-in charm, accented by the scent of Mari's apple crisp, cooling on the counter. It was a perfect setting for a happy, healthy family.

Upstairs, in Hannah's room, the boys were sprawled on a braided rug. It was a rare treat to play in their big sister's space. Hannah arranged her Barbies in a makeshift tea party, while Caleb and Josiah snapped together LEGO towers. "I hope I get the American Girl doll I asked for for Christmas," Hannah said as she moved one Barbie to the other side.

In the kitchen, Mari diced carrots for dinner. The radio hummed with Christian music, and her ears perked up at an announcement. "Join us in Portland for a Weekend to Remember marriage conference. No matter where your relationship stands—healthy, in crisis, or just beginning—we welcome

you and your spouse for a transformative experience." She paused, knife still, picturing a weekend away with Gary. Promises of a private, kid-free space, a chance to relax, and a focus on personal growth had caught her attention.

That evening, after the children were tucked into bed, Mari and Gary sat at the oak dining table as the glow of a single lamp cast soft shadows. Mari leaned forward, her hazel eyes bright. "Gary, I heard about a marriage conference on the radio today. It's in Portland, November 28, right after Thanksgiving."

Gary raised an eyebrow, setting down his coffee mug. "That's our anniversary weekend, Mari. You sure you wanna swap our Columbia Gorge Hotel trip for a conference?"

Mari nodded. "I know it's our special time, but they said it's for all couples—married or not, thriving or struggling. It could strengthen us, don't you think?"

Gary rubbed his chin. "Sounds like a lotta heart-to-heart stuff. We gotta spill our guts in front of strangers?"

Mari smiled, squeezing his hand. "No, the brochure said it's private—just us in our hotel room, working on our marriage. Let's pray about it and maybe ask Marni and her boyfriend. If they're in, it's a sign we should go."

Gary chuckled, his calloused fingers warm against hers. "Alright, if Marni and Tom sign up, I'm game. But I'm trusting you on the 'no public soul-baring' part."

They bowed their heads and asked for guidance. The next day, Mari's sister Marni called, her voice bubbling. "Tom and I are totally in for the conference! Separate rooms, time to focus on us—it's perfect. You guys going?"

Mari glanced at Gary, who was sprawled on the living room couch sorting through Hannah's schoolwork. He gave a thumbs-up. "That's our green light," Mari said, grinning. "We're in."

The following week, the two couples stepped into the Portland hotel's grand ballroom, where at least a hundred couples of all ages mingled—newlyweds beaming, older pairs with weary smiles, some eager, others bored or even angry. Mari's stomach knotted as she surveyed the crowd, her fingers tightening on Gary's arm. "I hope this is worth trading our anniversary getaway," she whispered, eyeing the tables of books lining the ballroom's walls.

Gary leaned close. "Better not be a 'share your secrets with the room' deal, Mari. I'm not built for that."

She nudged him, her smile teasing. "Relax, it's all private, just us. We agreed this could be good, right? Let's dive in."

Gary nodded, his reluctance softening. "Fine, let's see what they've got."

The emcee, a jovial man with a booming voice, opened the session. "Some of you might not be thrilled to be here," he said, scanning the room. "But I promise, by Sunday, you'll be glad you came."

A couple, Rick and Judy Taylor, took the stage, their unassuming appearance hiding a powerful story. "When we married, we had big dreams," Rick began, his hand on Judy's. "But life threw us a curveball. We've learned to lean on each other and on God to survive."

Mari scribbled furiously in the conference handbook, capturing prompts and ideas, while Gary listened intently, arms crossed with eyes fixed on the speakers. "Rick's a solid guy," he whispered to Mari during a break. "Not some soft-talker—a real man's man."

Mari nodded, flipping through her notes. "I like how they said to tackle issues head-on, not let them fester. Growing up, I saw how silence wrecked my mom's marriage. I don't want that for us."

The next morning, before the first session, Mari and Gary browsed the book tables. "At the end of the conference, we'll buy one book each," Gary said, scanning the titles. "You choose what you'd like, and I'll do the same."

Mari laughed, holding up a book on communication. "This one's mine. You?"

Gary picked up Rick Taylor's *When Life Is Changed Forever*. "This one. His story's got me hooked."

Mari's brow furrowed. "Isn't it too heavy? Losing a child . . . Gary, that's my worst nightmare."

Gary's face softened, his thoughts drifting to his brother's suicide. "I know, Mari. But I've seen loss tear people apart—my parents never recovered after my brother died. Maybe this'll show us how to hold on tighter."

The morning session outlined three threats to marriage: Invisible—Satan's distortions, blame-shifting, and control struggles; Internal—selfishness and blind spots; External—media and cultural influences undermining commitment. The presenters taught "fighting fair," offering practical conflict resolution tips. Mari reflected on her upbringing, while Gary thought of his father's drinking and the distance it created between his parents.

During a break, they met a couple from Vancouver. "We homeschool our kids," Mari shared. "Hannah's seven, Caleb's almost six, and Josiah is three. They keep us busy."

The wife smiled. "We've got two girls in public school, but we're considering homeschooling. How do you do it?"

"It's a juggling act," Gary said, grinning. "Mari's the mastermind. I'm just the UPS guy keeping Oregon's packages moving."

The afternoon session featured Rick and Judy's heart-wrenching story. Rick, then a pastor in Idaho, shared how their life changed at Pine Cove, a five-hundred-acre Christian camp in East Texas.

Judy's voice wavered as she recounted the day their son Kyle drowned. "It started like any other day," Judy said, her eyes distant. "The boys wanted to grab their tricycles by the dining hall, not far from our cabin. I never let them out of my sight, so this was rare."

She paused, her voice breaking. "They begged, 'Can we get our trikes? Just for a minute; we'll come right back.' I was eight months pregnant, exhausted. I said, 'Alright, three tricycles, go quick, we're leaving.' But then I got this awful feeling, like a weight in my chest. I ran outside, got in the van, started honking. They should've been back. Then I saw Brian, our middle son, crying, 'Mommy, they're dying in the water.'"

Mari gripped Gary's hand, her breath catching. Gary's jaw tightened as he pictured Hannah, Caleb, and Josiah.

Judy continued, "I ran to the pond, yelling for Brian to show me where they went in. I pulled Eric, our youngest, out, but I couldn't find Kyle. We rushed Eric to the hospital. He survived, defying the doctors' predictions of death or brain damage. But Kyle . . . his body was found later that day."

Rick took over, his voice steady but heavy. "Statistics say 80 percent of couples divorce after losing a child. We refused to let that be us. Judy needed to talk about it, over and over. I processed by writing a book, *When Life Is Changed Forever.*"

Judy added, "People ask if I'm 'back to normal.' I tell them it's like losing an arm—you learn to live, to write with your other hand, but you never stop missing that arm. Kyle was part of us. Time doesn't heal, but God comforts us, reshaping us into deeper people."

Mari wiped her eyes, whispering to Gary, "I can't imagine losing one of ours. It's too much."

Gary nodded, his voice low. "It's awful, but they're showing us how to keep going. That's strength."

The midafternoon session, "Let's Talk About Sex," brought lighter moments. Mari and Gary exchanged shy smiles, joining other couples in chuckling at the workbook questions.

"This part's not so bad," Gary teased, nudging Mari. "Maybe we'll learn something new."

Mari laughed, swatting his arm. "Behave, or I'll make you answer every question out loud."

On Sunday, the final day, the couples split into separate sessions for husbands and wives, discussing roles as parents and spouses. Gary felt a spark of excitement about being a better father, while Mari jotted down ideas for nurturing their marriage.

At the book table, Gary bought Rick's book, despite Mari's hesitation. "It's heavy, I know," he said, "but after my brother's death, I saw how grief can break you. This might help us stay strong."

Mari sighed, her fingers tracing her book's cover. "You're right. I've never faced loss like that. I just . . . I pray we never do."

As they returned home, the Vancouver sky glowed with November's crisp light, bathing their house's exterior in a warm hue. Mari and Gary felt renewed, their hearts brimming with fresh love and commitment, ready to face their future together.

Chapter 8

Trusting God with Our Fears

Don't fret or worry. Instead of worrying, pray.
Let petitions and praises shape your worries into prayers,
letting God know your concerns.
~ Philippians 4:6 MSG

The Malychewski home was hushed in the late November evening. The air carried the comforting aroma of the kitchen, infused with the soothing scent of chamomile tea steaming in two mugs on the oak dining table.

Mari and Gary sat close, the glow of a single lamp casting warm shadows across the room. The children were tucked into bed upstairs, their giggles from earlier play in Hannah's room now a memory.

Mari sipped her tea, her eyes bright with lingering excitement from the Weekend to Remember. "That conference was something else," she said, setting her mug down. "In the women's session, one of the leaders said if we pursue our relationship with God first, it strengthens our marriage. It hit me hard—I think sometimes I'm so focused on the kids, I don't let you dream. I want to be better about listening, really hearing you. I want us to be best friends, not just parents."

Gary nodded, "I hear you. In the men's session, they talked about being the head of the family—not by bossing everyone around, but by serving you. I've been guilty of trying to 'fix' things when you talk instead of just listening. I wanna understand what you need, Mari, not just jump to solutions."

Mari reached for his hand, her touch warm and steady. "That means a lot. I think we're already stronger for it, don't you?"

"Yeah," Gary said, squeezing her fingers. "Feels like we're starting fresh, like we did when we first got married."

Later, as they settled on the couch, Gary pulled out Rick Taylor's *When Life Is Changed Forever*. "When my brother Gerald took his life, it tore my parents apart. But Rick and Judy's story—they went through something unimaginable and came out stronger. You should read it."

Mari glanced at the book, her fingers tightening around her mug. "I don't know, Gary. I haven't faced death like you have. The idea of losing one of our kids—like their Kyle, only five, so close to Hannah's age—it's every parent's nightmare. I'm scared just thinking about it."

Gary set the book down, his eyes meeting hers. "I get it. When they told that story at the conference, about Kyle drowning and Eric nearly dying, I kept picturing Hannah, Caleb, and Josiah. Judy was a 'total mom,' like you—always watching the kids. And it still happened. But their faith, their marriage . . . they held on. I hope we'd be that strong. I pray we never have to find out."

Mari nodded, her voice soft. "My book from the conference says fears about the future can take over if we let them. I can't be hypervigilant all the time, watching the kids every second. I'm trying to trust God with my worries, but it's hard. Reading that book feels like tempting fate."

Gary leaned closer, his flannel sleeve brushing her arm. "I know it's tough. But maybe it's not about tempting fate—it's about learning how to lean on each other and God if the worst happens. I'll read it first, and we can talk about it. No pressure."

"Okay," Mari said, exhaling. "I'll look at it tomorrow. But only if you promise we'll talk through it together."

"Deal," Gary said, a small smile breaking through. "We're in this together, right?"

"Always," Mari replied, her eyes glistening as she leaned her head against his shoulder.

The following week, the house buzzed with Christmas preparations. The living room was a tangle of tinsel and half-strung lights, the bulletin board now adorned with Hannah's hand-cut paper snowflakes. The family was gearing up for a special outing to see The Nutcracker at a grand concert hall, their first time experiencing the ballet's magic together. Mari organized a cookie-baking day with the homeschool group, the kitchen soon to be filled with

the scent of gingerbread as Hannah, Caleb, Josiah, and their friends rolled dough and packed treats for the mailman, the paperboy, and the recycle and garbage people. It was a holiday tradition rooted in their faith and community at Vancouver Community Church.

As Mari tucked Hannah into bed one night, Hannah said, "Mama, are you and Daddy happier now?" her wide eyes searching.

Mari smiled, brushing a strand of hair from Hannah's face. "We are, sweetheart. We're learning how to love each other even better, and that makes us love you and your brothers even more."

Downstairs, Gary glanced at the open page of Rick's book, the words about grief and resilience echoing in his mind. He closed the book, whispering a prayer for strength, trusting God to guide them through whatever lay ahead.

Chapter 9

Treats for All

Once, even if just for a heartbeat, everything was perfect.
~ Jodi Picoult

On Monday, December 15, the Malychewski home pulsed with the joy of a baking day. The house, its broad eaves adorned with a string of twinkling Christmas lights, stood inviting under a cloudy morning sky, a single brass lantern glowing beside the front door. Inside, the living room radiated coziness, with morning light filtering through heavy linen curtains onto a well-worn rug and a side table strewn with coloring books and a jumble of puzzle pieces. A narrow hallway, its walls lined with the children's finger-painted artwork, led to a lively kitchen where rolling pins and cookie cutters were piled high, the air thick with the promise of gingerbread and sugar.

Mari, dressed in faded jeans and a cozy gray sweatshirt, set out ingredients on the counter. Hannah, seven, bounced excitedly, while Caleb and Josiah, her younger brothers, rummaged through a tin of sprinkles.

"Mommy, can we make star cookies for the mailman?" Hannah asked, holding up a cutter.

"Stars, angels, whatever you want," Mari said, smiling as she measured flour. "Just keep the sprinkles on the table, not the floor, okay?"

Caleb piped up, "I want to give the paperboy a snowman cookie!"

Josiah giggled, his hands already dusted with sugar. "And a big one for the garbage man!"

Mari laughed, wiping her hands on her apron. "We'll make plenty for the mailman, the paperboy, and the recycle and garbage folks. Now, let's get rolling!"

Midmorning, Mari bundled the kids into the van to return some borrowed books to the home of a friend across town. The drive through Vancouver's quiet streets, lined with bare maples and twinkling holiday lights, was filled with the children's chatter about their cookie plans. At the friend's house, Mari chatted with Mike, a father in the group, while the kids played nearby.

"Homeschooling's a challenge," Mike said, leaning against his doorframe. "But it's worth it, right?"

"Definitely," Mari replied, her braid swaying as she nodded. "Though keeping up with three kids sometimes feels like herding cats."

Mike chuckled, then added, "Been a policeman for ten years now. Seen a lot, but nothing beats coming home to my kids."

Mari smiled. "Good to know we've got folks like you out there." They chatted a bit longer before Mari herded the kids back to the van.

On the drive home, the kids' voices filled the van—Hannah planning cookie decorations, Caleb singing a jumbled Christmas carol, Josiah mimicking him. Mari's thoughts drifted, her hands steady on the wheel as she reflected on disturbing ideas she'd had the week before. She had spoken to her mother-in-law about them. "I can't shake this feeling that something bad's coming—I don't know what or who. Would you pray about this?"

The unease gnawed at her, but she pushed it aside, focusing on the road and the kids' laughter. Just nerves, she told herself. Too much to do before Christmas.

Back at the Malychewski home, the kitchen became a flour-dusted wonderland. The counters were a mess of dough scraps and icing smudges as Hannah carefully pressed star-shaped cutters into the dough, Caleb smeared icing with a spatula, and Josiah sneaked a cookie when he thought Mari wasn't looking.

"No more!" Mari said, catching him with a grin as the kids begged for another taste. "Those are for our delivery people, not your tummies. Bed early tonight—you've worked hard."

The next morning, Hannah bounded downstairs and plopped into a chair in front of her breakfast. "I can't wait to take the cookies to everyone!" she exclaimed, nearly spilling her cereal.

Mari, stirring her coffee, raised a finger. "Settle down, sweetheart. Eat your cereal, put your bowl in the sink. We've got schoolwork first, then we'll deliver the cookies."

The children scattered to dress, then gathered at the oak dining table for lessons, their books spread across its scarred surface. Josiah, too young for formal schoolwork, built LEGO towers on the floor.

"Mommy, will we have a cake for my birthday?" Caleb asked, his pencil pausing over a math worksheet. He was looking forward to his sixth birthday the following week.

Mari smiled, ruffling his hair. "Of course, Caleb. We'll have a big cake, and everyone will come to celebrate—Grandma, Grandpa, maybe even Aunt Marni and Tom."

"Yay!" Caleb beamed, then turned to Hannah. "Can we play The Nutcracker game after schoolwork? I wanna be the Mouse King!"

Hannah giggled, her eyes bright. "Only if I get to be Clara!"

Mari watched them, her heart swelling, but that nagging unease from her previous scary thoughts lingered. She glanced out the kitchen window, where the Vancouver sky was heavy with gray clouds, a chill seeping through the glass. The memory of Gary's near accident in Vernonia months ago flickered in her mind, and she whispered a quick prayer for protection.

Chapter 10

A Day No Parent Wants to Face

The LORD is close to the brokenhearted
and saves those who are crushed in spirit.

~ Psalm 34:18

G ary glanced at the clock as the alarm blared at 5:30 A.M. on December 16, 1997. An inexplicable agitation churned in his gut. What's wrong with me? he thought, rubbing his eyes. Mari lay motionless beside him, her warm, gentle expression peaceful in sleep. Gary slipped out of bed and stumbled into the bathroom.

The hot shower did little to quell the agitation in his gut. He dressed in his UPS uniform, the fabric stiff and familiar, and grabbed his packed lunch from the refrigerator. Back in the bedroom, he kissed Mari goodbye before he headed out the front door.

Driving through the farmlands west of Portland, Gary tuned the radio to his favorite Christian station. The pastor's voice filled the cab, speaking on a beloved verse: "Be still, and know that I am God." The words wrapped around him, calming his earlier irritation. Lord, help me be still, he prayed, the fields blurring past in the dim light.

At home, Mari stirred awake around 7:00 as the house came alive with the children's chatter. Dressed in jeans and a red sweatshirt, she padded to the kitchen, where Hannah chattered about the cookies baked the day before. Caleb and Josiah rubbed sleepy eyes, eager for breakfast.

"Mommy, can we deliver the cookies today?" Hannah asked as Mari spooned oatmeal into their bowls.

"Soon, sweetheart," Mari replied, ruffling Hannah's hair. "After schoolwork."

The kitchen was a jumble of tins filled with stars and angels sprinkled with red and green sugar. Mari felt a fleeting peace, anchored by the routine after the emotional marriage conference and fears stirred by Rick Taylor's book. Still, her thoughts from before echoed. Something bad's coming. She pushed them aside, focusing on the children's chatter.

Just before 9:00, the rumble of the recycling truck roared through the alley behind the house. Hannah's eyes lit up. "I'll give them now!" she cried, grabbing a tin of cookies and dashing for the back door.

"Wait, Hannah! Let me come with you!" Mari called as she set down her coffee mug. The door slammed, and Hannah's small figure vanished into the alley. She called out to her, "Hannah, no! Wait for me!" Hannah kept running, intent on getting the recycle driver his Christmas cookies she and her two brothers had made.

Oh, Hannah, he can't see you. Mari's heart was beating as if she'd run a five-minute mile.

"Hannah!" she screamed as she ran across the backyard toward the alley. The screech of brakes tore through her soul.

Hannah's body lay still and filled Mari's vision. All was silent except one voice screaming like a banshee! Who was that? Then she realized it was she herself screaming. "Oh God. This can't be real. Please. Please don't let it be." Mari ran back into the house, grabbed the remote phone, and punched in 911.

The calm voice on the phone asked, "Emergency, please?"

She blurted, "My daughter just got run over by the recycle truck."

The operator asked her to do some lifesaving act that she knew would do no good to help her girl.

She yelled, "She was run over by a truck!"

Back outside, she grabbed Hannah's lifeless hand, snot running down her face, tears blurring her vision. Mari shivered in shock, hardly able to breathe.

The driver was at the side of the alley, kneeling, his head in his hands.

The idling of the truck and the wail of approaching sirens saturated the alley—fire trucks, ambulances, police. Vancouver police officer Mike Knotts, whom Mari had met the day before, knelt beside her.

"Mari, it's me," he said softly, his eyes full of compassion. "I'm so sorry. What can I do?"

"Call Gary," she choked out, tears streaming. "I need him here."

As Mike dialed, Mari called Pastor Neal Curtiss. "Neal, you have to come. Hannah's dead!" she cried.

When Pastor Curtiss pulled up to the curb, Mari collapsed into his arms. "Is my little girl in heaven?" she whispered in a fragile voice.

"Absent from the body, present with the Lord," he said, holding her tightly. "Hannah's with Jesus, safe and whole."

Mari nodded, sobbing. "The conference we went to said most marriages fail after losing a child. I don't want that for us."

"We'll pray for strength," he assured, leading her inside.

Meanwhile, Gary's phone chimed with a text from his shop steward: Meet the boss at McDonald's.

What's going on? he wondered, the morning's agitation roaring back. Heart pounding, he dialed home. "Mari, what's wrong?"

"Hannah's dead!" she screamed.

"What?" he gasped, pulling over, the radio pastor's sermon on stillness now a cruel echo.

Mari recounted the horror between sobs—the truck, the screech, their daughter's body. Gary's mind reeled, flashing to the Vernonia near-accident months ago, the little girl on her bike so like Hannah. Not my girl, he thought, tears falling.

At McDonald's, his boss's grave face confirmed the worst. "Jump in. I'll drive you home."

The fifty-minute drive from North Plains to Vancouver was torture. How do we survive this? The conference warned us—loss destroys marriages. Not us, Lord, Gary prayed, picturing Hannah's laughter, her excitement over the cookies.

Vehicles clogged the street—fire trucks, police, coroner's car, a TV station van parked prominently in front of the house. Larry Trimble, Gary's friend, greeted him with a wordless hug, eyes brimming.

"I need to talk to the driver," Gary said, voice steady despite the storm inside.

In the alley, police surrounded Kris, the driver, following standard procedures.

Gary approached, compassion overriding anger. "This could happen to anyone," he told Kris, tapping his shoulder. "I forgive you."

Kris nodded, head down, silent. Gary knew that feeling of guilt—he'd carried it since Vernonia.

Inside, Mari paced, muttering, "I should have stopped her. It's my fault."

When Gary entered, she fell into his arms. "Oh, Gary, what can we do?" she sobbed.

"I'm here. We'll hold on and never let go," he whispered, wrapping her in his strength.

In their bedroom, away from the crowd, Mari retold the nightmare, her voice breaking. "The conference said child loss tears couples apart."

"We won't let it," Gary vowed, cupping her face. "I believe even if you were holding Hannah in your arms, God would have taken her. It was her time." He prayed softly, "Lord, hold our marriage. Don't let this divide us. Amen."

Friends and family gathered, their faces heavy with grief. Someone brewed coffee, another brought sandwiches, small acts of care in the chaos.

When Gary's brother Presley arrived, their old rift dissolved in a silent embrace, united by new grief.

Mari glanced at the clock. "It's four o'clock! I haven't fed the boys!" she cried, jumping up.

"Someone's taking care of them," Gary said gently.

"No, it's my job," she insisted, voice trembling. In the living room, Caleb and Josiah built LEGO structures with their friends. Caleb looked up. "Mommy, will I still have my birthday party?"

Mari knelt, hugging him, her heart breaking. "Yes, honey. Presents, cake, everything." Caleb nodded, adding a piece to his airport, shielded by his innocence.

As evening fell, friends offered quiet support—coffee brewed, sandwiches shared, prayers whispered. Exhausted, Gary and Mari ate food tasteless to them, tucked the boys into bed with extra kisses, and retreated. In their bedroom, they clung together, raw with grief, becoming one flesh in desperate comfort. Their tears mingled as sleep took them.

But the nightmare was not over—planning Hannah's memorial, three days away, was a final goodbye no parent could fathom.

Chapter 11

From the Driver to the Owners

*I follow three rules: Do the right thing, do the best you can,
and always show people you care.*

~ Lou Holtz

The Vancouver alley had been quiet that December morning in 1997, the air sharp with the scent of wet pavement. For Kris Wright, a twenty-three-year-old recycle truck driver, it was just another shift—until a single moment changed everything. Twenty-seven years later, the memory of that day would linger, a wound that never fully healed for anyone who was involved.

Kris had been on the job for six months, long enough to earn his own route in an older Vancouver neighborhood. Neat rows of houses faced the street, their sidewalks leading to welcoming front doors, but the real work happened in the alleys, where garages and trash bins waited. His truck, a 1997 model without auto-braking, required him to stand and drive on the right side of the cab, working control levers to lift bins into the hopper. He'd drive down one side of the alley, turn around, and come back for the bins on the other side.

The Malychewski house was his first stop on the right side of the alley. Kris knew the family, not by name, but by the little girl who'd run out with a tin of cookies on holidays.

"She was always so eager," he'd later tell me, his voice soft. "Bright eyes, maybe seven, always leading her younger siblings. She'd hand me that tin of cookies with her mom trailing behind, smiling. It made the job feel human."

That morning, Hannah had heard the familiar rumble of Kris's truck. She'd grabbed a tin of cookies, clutching the metal container, and darted out the back gate.

"I was working the levers," Kris said, his voice breaking as he recounted it. "You look back to line up the bin with the hopper. It's routine—lift, dump, set down. I eased the truck forward, and then . . . a bump." His stomach had lurched. He'd heard a scream, cut the engine, and leapt out, boots crunching on the gravel.

There was Hannah, crumpled in the alley, her tin of cookies spilled open in the dirt.

Her mother knelt beside her, clutching her tiny hand, her screams tearing through the morning air. "Hannah! Hannah, please!" she sobbed, her face streaked with tears.

"I never saw her," Kris whispered as he recounted the event, his hands trembling. "The cab's too high, and she was so small. She came from the left, and I was focused on the right." He'd stumbled to the side of the alley, retching, his mind replaying the thud. He climbed back into the truck, hands shaking as he radioed dispatch, then dialed 911. "There's been an accident," he managed, his voice hollow. "A little girl . . . the house on 'I' Street."

Kris was too shaken to drive. A police officer led him to the back of the Operations Manager's vehicle, where a male grief counselor joined him, asking gentle questions. Kris answered in a daze, the counselor's notepad blurring through his tears.

"He prayed with me," Kris recalled, his voice catching. "He gave me a handkerchief—I still have it." Later, his mother picked him up to take him to a clinic for a mandatory drug test. "Of course it was clean," Kris said. "I loved my job. I'd never mess it up like that."

That evening, Kris had sat slumped at his mother's kitchen table, the weight of the day pressing down. His mother and stepfather sat close, their hands hovering, unsure how to comfort him. Across the table were Ron Mittelstaedt, Waste Connections's CEO who'd flown hours to be there, and Darrell Chambliss, who was the COO and the temporary Vancouver site manager. The room was heavy with grief.

"Tell us what happened, Kris," Ron said gently, as he draped his suit jacket over the chair.

Kris's voice cracked as he recounted again how his focus had been on the opposite side of Hannah's approach. He buried his face in his hands. "I saw her lying there, and I knew . . . I knew she was gone. Her mom was screaming, holding her hand. I couldn't move. I just . . . I vomited by the road, then called dispatch."

Ron leaned forward, his eyes steady but kind. "We don't hold you responsible, Kris. We'll investigate every detail, but for now, you need time. Take a few days. We'll set you up with someone to talk to, if you want."

"I'm fine," Kris stammered, though his red-rimmed eyes said otherwise. "The counselor prayed with me. I just . . . I want to go back to work." He paused, his voice barely above a whisper. "I'd like to go to the funeral, but . . . would they even want me there?"

"We'll go with you," Ron said without hesitation.

Darrell nodded. "Let's give it a couple of days, Kris. You need to process this."

Ron and Darrell stood, their chairs scraping softly against the linoleum. "Don't bottle this up," Ron added. "Promise us that."

Kris nodded, hunched over, his head between his hands as the men left the house.

Outside, Darrell turned to Ron as they reached the car. "Now what?"

Ron's jaw tightened. "We visit the Malychewski's tonight."

"Are you sure?" Darrell asked, his voice low.

"It's the right thing to do," Ron said firmly. He'd grown up in a Christian home, the Golden Rule etched into his core: Do to others as you would have them do to you. He thought of his own children and his chest ached. "If this happened to one of my kids, I'd want someone to face me, to show they cared." He glanced at the darkening Vancouver sky. "And find out which funeral home is handling the arrangements. We'll cover the expenses."

That evening, Ron and Darrell walked up the sidewalk to the Malychewski home. Through the front window, they glimpsed a living room glowing with Christmas cheer—a tree strung with popcorn garlands, paper chains draped across the mantel, lights twinkling. But the scene inside was somber: friends and family sat in a tight circle around Gary and Mari, their faces etched with grief.

Gary opened the door, his eyes bloodshot, his flannel shirt rumpled. He stepped onto the porch, closing the door behind him.

"Mr. Malychewski," Ron began, his voice steady but soft, "we're so sorry for this terrible accident. We can't imagine what you're going through."

Gary nodded, his gaze distant. "I understand," he said, his voice barely above a whisper. "I can't talk now. My wife . . . she needs me." He turned, closing the door softly, leaving the men standing in the chill evening air.

They drove to the funeral home, where Ron spoke quietly with the director. "We'll cover all expenses for Hannah's funeral," he said. "But let the offer come from you. It feels more personal that way."

In two days, they would see the Malychewskis again—at a funeral no one could have prepared for.

Chapter 12

The Memorial Service

Grief is not a disorder, a disease, or a sign of weakness.
It is an emotional, physical and spiritual necessity; the price you pay for love.
The only cure for grief is to grieve.
~ Rabbi Earl A. Grollman

Friday, December 19, 1997, dawned a breezy, gray day in the upper thirties, the heavy clouds mirroring the hearts of those gathering at Vancouver Community Church. The parking lot overflowed with cars, a KATU News van parked obtrusively among them, its bright logo jarring against the somber mood. No rain fell, but the air hung thick with mist.

Inside, the church buzzed with quiet sorrow; the quiet hum of whispered prayers mingled with the murmur of mourners and the scent of lilies. Mourners' faces were etched with grief and quiet relief that this loss wasn't theirs, though they longed to ease the Malychewskis' pain with hugs that could never suffice.

Only One could truly comfort, and he was present, holding the family as they walked, talked, and wept.

The family chose not to have Hannah's body at the service, but her treasures filled a table at the front: her favorite dollies; a pink Bible with "Hannah" engraved in gold, soon to be placed in her arms at burial; a soccer ball and uniform, dedicated to her memory by the 1997 soccer club. Photographs lined the table—Hannah alone, grinning with her bright eyes, and with her family, her brothers Caleb and Josiah clinging to her. A handwritten note read, "I love

my family and I love my friends. The End." Hannah, seven and soon to turn eight, had loved to sing, practicing with the children's choir for their Sunday performance. She loved and was loved, and the packed sanctuary on a workday afternoon confirmed it.

Local reporters and TV cameras hovered at the edges, their presence an unwelcome intrusion. A KATU reporter, wiping his eyes, whispered to Pastor Neal Curtiss, "I've covered services for twenty years, but this one's got me crying."

Mari, seated in the front pew, gazed at the table with the pink Bible, picturing Hannah singing like an angel. Pastor Neal's words from Tuesday echoed: Hannah's with Jesus, safe and whole. But the family she left behind was shattered. Mari's journal lay open nearby, her words raw: "I have loved you like no other. You were a first to a lot of people. My first child. A first niece, cousin, or grandchild to some. You got me started on my parenting journey. And now, with your death, I face my first loss of someone so close."

Caleb, turning six tomorrow, had written in wobbly letters, "Dear Hannah, I look forward to playing with you when I get to heaven."

Josiah, three, clutched an action figure, too young to grasp the void.

Pastor Neal took the pulpit, his voice steady yet heavy. "Hannah was a child who loved—her brothers, Caleb and Josiah, her family, her friends, everyone she met. Jesus promises to heal the brokenhearted and bandage their wounds. Stay close to this family. This is a long journey. Listen to them. Pray for them." He looked at Gary and Mari, seated in the front pew, hands clasped tightly. "You will seek answers for why this happened, but you may never find them. God has a purpose, though we don't know it, perhaps never will. Your marriage will face deep waters. Grieve in your own way, without expectations of each other. Your faith will be tested, but you are not alone."

The congregation sang Hannah's favorite songs—"Jesus Loves Me," "Away in a Manger"—their voices trembling. Gary, holding Josiah, felt Hannah's absence acutely, remembering how she'd watch over her brothers and how her laughter filled their home.

In the back, Kris Wright, the driver, sat rigid, flanked by Ron Mittelstaedt, who'd stayed since the accident, and Darrell Chambliss, to honor Hannah. Kris's hands trembled. He'd dreaded this moment, unsure if the family would welcome him, his guilt a constant shadow since Tuesday's tragedy.

Pastor Neal's voice softened. "Is the driver of the truck here?"

Kris lifted his head, meeting the pastor's eyes, his heart pounding.

"Would you mind coming to the front?"

Kris rose slowly, legs unsteady, as Ron gave him a reassuring nod.

Gary stood, Josiah in his arms, and faced Kris. The grieving father stepped forward, his eyes brimming, and pulled Kris into a hug. "I don't hold any grudge against you," he said softly, his voice steady despite the grief. "I know it wasn't your fault."

The embrace lingered, Kris's shoulders shaking, as the congregation began to sing "Amazing Grace," raising their voices in a wave of shared sorrow.

Mari watched, tears streaming, her hand on Caleb's shoulder. The room blurred as mourners lined up to offer condolences, some seeking comfort from the family they meant to console. Exhausted from sleep-broken nights, Gary and Mari nodded and hugged, their strength waning but their faith holding.

The next day they would celebrate Caleb's sixth birthday, a celebration tinged with grief. On Monday, the graveside service awaited—the final goodbye to Hannah's shattered body, a moment no parent could fathom.

Chapter 13

A Birthday Song out of Tune

The shattering of a heart when being broken is the loudest quiet ever.
~ Carroll Bryant

Saturday, December 20, 1997, dawned breezy and gray. Caleb, bursting with the excitement of turning six, bounced into their bedroom early that morning. "Mommy! Daddy! My birthday's today!" he exclaimed, clutching his new soccer ball under his arm. Then he flopped down, voice softening. "But I'm sad 'cause Hannah can't come."

Mari and Gary forced smiles, their eyes red from sleepless nights since the fateful Tuesday the week before. The living room glowed with Christmas cheer—popcorn garlands on the tree, paper chains draped across the mantel—but the room felt bleak without Hannah's laughter. How do we celebrate? Mari thought, her chest tight, recalling Pastor Neal's words: Your faith will be tested, but you are not alone.

Family members arrived with presents wrapped in bright paper, though their faces were strained with forced cheer. Caleb's soccer team buddies filled the room, their chatter mingling with the scent of vanilla cake and melting candles. The children oohed and aahed as Caleb tore open gifts—a model airplane, a puzzle, a stuffed bear—yet Hannah's absence loomed. She wasn't there to orchestrate games or nudge Caleb to open the "best" present first. The joy felt out of tune, like an orchestra with each musician playing a different song, off-key and strained.

Mari lit the candles with trembling hands and Gary led a shaky "Happy Birthday." Caleb beamed as he blew out the six candles, but Mari's gaze drifted to the tin of star-and-angel cookies on the counter, untouched since Tuesday's tragedy. A condolence card from Waste Connections, signed by Ron Mittelstaedt, sat among the gifts, a quiet reminder of the company's support.

As evening fell, Mari tucked Caleb and Josiah into bed, extra kisses lingering on their foreheads. Caleb clutched his new stuffed bear, whispering, "I miss Hannah."

Josiah, with an action figure gripped in his hand, slept soundly.

In their bedroom, Mari and Gary tried to sleep, but grief kept them awake, their whispered prayers echoing their vow earlier that week.

Sunday morning, the boys' laughter filled the living room as they played with Caleb's new toys, but Hannah's voice was missing.

"Should we go to church?" Mari asked, her voice heavy.

"I guess," Gary replied, rubbing his eyes. "It might be good for the boys." Their faith, battered but unbroken, urged them forward, a faint echo of the radio sermon Gary had heard Tuesday: Be still, and know that I am God.

Mari called out, "Boys, let's get dressed. It's church today." In the kitchen, she set out cereal and milk.

They arrived at the church late, slipping into a back pew to avoid the front where they'd sat for Hannah's memorial. Mari's heart screamed, I only want Hannah!

Pastor Neal Curtiss caught their eyes, offering a gentle nod, hoping his sermon on hope would be a quiet balm.

After the service, familiar faces and strangers surrounded them, hugs and condolences pressing in. Gary held Josiah, his action figure dangling, while Mari gripped Caleb's hand, their grief raw beneath polite nods. We need to be alone, Gary thought, longing for quiet.

At home, the boys built LEGO towers while Mari and Gary sat close, hands entwined. A quiet day, just the four of them, was all they could manage before tomorrow's graveside service—the final goodbye to Hannah.

Chapter 14

Goodbye, Hannah

Joy has left our hearts; our dancing has turned to mourning.
~ Lamentations 5:15 NLT

Monday, December 22, 1997, was anything but a typical December day in Vancouver. The family drove to the funeral home, where they picked up Hannah's pink coffin, so small it broke their hearts anew.

Gary and the funeral director carefully slid it into the back of the van, the wood cold under their fingers. With Hannah's body now in the van, the family of five—Gary, Mari, Caleb, Josiah, and Hannah—were together for the last time as they began their drive.

The van was quiet, no voices filling the void. Hannah wasn't there to entertain her brothers or interpret Josiah's words, her role as his translator silenced. Mari stared out the window, her thoughts on the pink Bible with "Hannah" engraved in gold, now resting with her daughter in the coffin, a sacred touch from Friday's memorial. Gary gripped the steering wheel as they headed to Goldendale, Washington, 125 miles away, for the 11:00 A.M. graveside service.

An hour and a half later, they arrived at the cemetery, patches of snow dusting the grave markers, the sun breaking through in fleeting rays, the temperature just above freezing. A slight breeze that rustled the bare trees carried the faint crunch of snow underfoot.

Mari and Gary sat with the boys in their laps. Josiah gripped his action figure, its plastic edges worn from constant holding. The breaths of family and

a few close friends who stood behind them were visible in the chill air.

Pastor Neal Curtiss began, his voice steady with Scripture. "Hannah is in heaven. Jesus said, 'I am the resurrection and the life. The one who believes in me will live, even though they die.' Hannah believed in Jesus as her personal Savior. She was a living example of a child of God." He paused, meeting Mari's eyes. "Mari told me that every morning, she and the children studied the Bible together. One morning, Hannah prayed and asked Jesus to come into her heart. Her faith was real. She stood up for others when they needed an advocate."

Pastor Neal continued, "Paul wrote, 'And now, dear brothers and sisters, we want you to know what will happen to the believers who have died so you will not grieve like people who have no hope.' Hannah is with Jesus right now, in complete joy, not suffering. But Gary and Mari miss her terribly."

As he closed in prayer, sobs broke the silence. "Oh God, please be with Gary and Mari—and the rest of us as we say goodbye to Hannah. Soothe our grieving hearts as you promise: 'He will wipe every tear from their eyes, and there will be no more death or sorrow or crying or pain.' Comfort the brokenhearted and rescue those whose spirits are crushed, as Gary's and Mari's are now. We commit them to you, the only one who can truly comfort. In Jesus's name, amen."

Pastor Neal walked to Gary and Mari and hugged them tightly. Mari approached the small coffin and wrapped her arms around it, her sobs echoing across the hillside as if they'd never stop. Gary joined her, his arm around her shoulders, tears streaming. Caleb stared at the coffin, his new stuffed bear dangling, while Josiah, clutching his action figure, looked to Mari, confused. The finality was beyond their grasp.

Family and friends passed by, offering hugs and whispered words as their eyes reflected shared sorrow. Slowly, the cars departed the windswept cemetery, the Malychewski van lingering last. A small Baptist church nearby provided a small comfort, the warmth of soup and bread. Mari and Gary ate mechanically, their hearts too heavy for hunger. As they drove back to Vancouver, Mari glanced at the empty road behind, whispering, "Goodbye, Hannah," one last time.

When they pulled up to their house that evening, a living blue-spruce Christmas tree stood on the front porch, adorned with delicate angel ornaments and twinkling lights, left by Christian friends. Its soft glow pierced the dusk, a silent gift of hope amid their grief, a reminder that Hannah's light lingered.

Hannah's final resting place
at Mountain View Cemetery

Christmas tree adorned with angels
waiting on the porch

Chapter 15

Challenges of Grief

We miss Hannah so terribly much.
There are no feelings or words to express our overwhelming grief.
~ Mari Malychewski

By spring 1998, the yellow forsythia bush outside the Malychewski home bloomed, its golden hues vibrant in the sunlight that broke through the clouds. Months had passed since Hannah's death on that fateful Tuesday, but the ache lingered like a shadow, or as neighbor Janice put it, "a hole in their heart that is just Hannah size."

The family stayed close to home through spring and summer, as if venturing too far or meeting strangers might unravel their fragile hold on each other. Outings were confined to visits with extended family.

Mari, once the outgoing heart of the neighborhood, withdrew into herself.

"Mari confided that there were difficulties in her and Gary's marriage," said neighbor Sarah, "asking me to pray for them."

Mari declined most invitations, sometimes accepting only to cancel at the last moment, fearing a sudden breakdown that might unsettle others. Her days with Caleb and Josiah were mechanical—helping Caleb with his homeschool curriculum, ensuring Josiah's playtime—but her spirit was heavy. She'd catch herself frozen, replaying Hannah's dash to the alley, guilt gnawing at her because she had not stopped her.

Neighborhood gatherings grew rare, the street quieter without Hannah's

bright presence. Sympathy cards still arrived, piling in a box Mari kept by her bedside, some containing unexpected sums of money tucked inside, their anonymous generosity a mystery she couldn't unravel. She reread them often, many from strangers moved by the tragedy. Their words were a bittersweet reminder of the community's care. Yet the unyielding weight in her heart remained.

While Josiah pushed a toy truck across the floor and Caleb worked on math, Mari pored over her Bible, its pages worn from desperate searches for solace. She reflected on the Weekend to Remember, realizing God had fortified her and Gary, however slightly, for this loss. Still, sorrow clung to them like damp Vancouver mist. "I wish I could just talk to Judy," Mari told her sister Marni, longing for the mother from the conference who'd lost her son to drowning.

Hearing this, Marni tracked down Judy Taylor's contact information.

On January 11, 1998, what would have been Hannah's eighth birthday, Judy called to talk.

"Will I ever feel good again?" Mari asked, her voice breaking.

"I'll be honest," Judy said. "This will hurt for a long time. Sometimes I wanted to die, but I had three other children to care for. When Kyle drowned, I was eight months pregnant with Kelly. The exhaustion wasn't just pregnancy—it was missing Kyle. I kept thinking I shouldn't have let the boys play outside, blaming myself endlessly, though Rick never blamed me."

"I know," Mari sobbed. "I feel that guilt too." Their shared pain forged a bond no one else in Mari's circle could fully grasp.

"It'll be a long time before you feel 'normal,' " Judy continued. "You can't go back to before. Your family's different now. Are you tired all the time?"

"Yes," Mari whispered. "I forget to feed the boys, lose track of things. No one understands, except . . . you."

"I do. Many friends won't get it. Let them help, but give yourself space. Don't shut out Gary—he's hurting, too. This takes time." Judy's voice cracked, recalling her son. "Kyle's been gone nineteen years, and it still aches, but the Lord is near. He understands."

The call didn't lift Mari's sorrow, but her burden was slightly eased by sharing it with someone who understood.

One afternoon, one of the many people who stopped by their home told them about "Bereaved Parents Share," a Christian organization offering

comfort through monthly mailers. This was vital in 1998 when internet grief resources were scarce. Mari avidly read through the newsletter every month, finding comfort through other grieving parents' words.

Gary, in his own words, described himself as "a mess." Grief overwhelmed him, forcing him to pull over in his UPS truck to sob, tears blurring the rural roads. After a few minutes, he'd dry his eyes and press on, each delivery draining his focus. The Teamsters' Union offered time off, and Gary took sick days whenever he could.

Caleb buried himself in homeschool work, his stuffed bear—a gift from his sixth birthday—clutched tightly as a reminder of Hannah and as a shield against the quiet. Josiah played with his trucks and action figures, his speech still muddled without Hannah's translation.

"Caleb and Josiah missed their sister, who was ringleader and cheerleader, spreading sunshine in their lives," a neighbor reflected.

Friends Mike and Kim added, "When Hannah was killed, a part of her family died too. Her death had a painful effect on everyone who knew her."

The community saw strength beneath the Malychewskis' grief.

"Mari's love for children was obvious," a friend recalled. "She never yelled, correcting them quietly. The boys' eyes lit up when they spoke of Gary's playful nature."

Another noted, "Underneath it all, there's a deep faith in Mari and Gary, a respect for each other as a couple and protective spirit as parents."

Yet, as Stephanie said, "There will always be a void. Gary and Mari are strong, pushing through this tragedy, teaching their children resilience."

As spring warmed Vancouver, Mari's longing for another child grew, a flicker of hope to ease Hannah's absence.

"Why did we ever think we'd be done with having children?" she asked Gary one evening, the scent of blooming lilacs drifting through the open window.

"We had a girl and two boys," Gary replied, his voice heavy. "We thought that was enough."

"But now we only have two," Mari whispered. "Can we find out if the vasectomy can be reversed?"

Through a couple from the Weekend to Remember, they found Dr. Ellis, a urologist offering discounts for reversals to couples facing changed circumstances.

"I can do the surgery in April," he said, the sterile hum of his office a stark contrast to their grief. "But there are no guarantees you'll conceive."

The anonymous money from the sympathy cards, carefully saved, covered the cost, a quiet providence Mari couldn't trace.

In April 1998, Gary underwent the reversal with cautious hope. Caleb and Josiah, unaware of the surgery's weight, played soccer with Gary when he returned, their excitement providing brief joy.

One summer evening, after a soccer game with the boys, bedtime stories, and prayers, Mari and Gary collapsed into bed, exhausted.

"I'm pregnant," Mari said, her voice trembling with joy and fear.

"Are you sure?" Gary asked. "The doctor said it might take a year."

"He was wrong. This baby's due next March."

Mari chronicled her journey in the "Bereaved Parents Share" newsletter:

> We miss Hannah so terribly much. There are no feelings or words to express our overwhelming grief. It is hard to believe it has been a year. I went from a house of men and a lovely little lady—to a house of men. I love them each dearly, but no child can ever replace my daughter who died. God has blessed us with a fourth pregnancy, due in March 1999. If it's a boy, his name will be Samuel Jonathan. If it's a girl, she will be named Ruth Elizabeth. Thanksgiving this year was hard. . . . Little did we know that last Thanksgiving would be our last major holiday spent together. It made me sad to think of the joys and fun I am missing and will never again have.

In the spring of 1999, Samuel Jonathan was born, his tiny cries filling the hospital room. Caleb and Josiah peered at their brother, Caleb clutching his bear, Josiah his truck, their eyes wide with wonder.

"He's little, like me," Josiah said, his speech clearer now.

Mari and Gary, holding Samuel, felt a fragile hope, Mari's written thought echoing through their minds: No child can ever replace my daughter who died.

Chapter 16

Joy in Pain

I have told you all this so that you may have peace in me.
Here on earth you will have many trials and sorrows.
But take heart, because I have overcome the world.

~ John 16:33 NLT

By 2000, the Malychewski family had moved to a larger home in Camas, Washington, nestled among rolling hills where wildflowers bloomed and the sound of children's chatter echoed through a natural playground of fir trees and open fields. Gary continued his UPS deliveries, now on the Washington side of the Columbia River, the steady rhythm of his routes a calming presence. Mari homeschooled Caleb, now nine, and Josiah, six, their desks cluttered with books and projects, while Samuel, a toddling one-year-old, babbled nearby.

By 2004, the family had grown to eight with the births of Gideon in 2001 and Abigail in 2004, each name drawn from the Bible—Samuel, for Hannah's prayer answered in 1 Samuel 1:19–28; Gideon, the faithful warrior of Judges 6–8; and Abigail, the wise woman of 1 Samuel 25:2–42. Yet one remained in heaven, Hannah's absence a constant undercurrent.

One spring afternoon, Mari watched Samuel and Josiah chase each other across the grassy yard. Caleb, kicking a soccer ball Hannah once loved, joined them, his focus sharp as he dribbled past his brother. Mari's heart lifted, then sank, imagining Hannah, who'd be ten, leading her brothers as their "second mother." The younger children wouldn't be here if she were alive, she thought, the bittersweet truth piercing her.

After moving to Camas, the family joined a small church near their new home. One Sunday in 2004, as the congregation sang "It Is Well with My Soul," Mari cradled newborn Abigail, and her tiny breaths brought hope.

Pastor Neal, though now miles away in Vancouver, remained a steady voice, his occasional calls offering comfort as he had at Hannah's graveside service.

A Camas neighbor, lingering after the service, squeezed Mari's hand, whispering, "Your strength inspires us."

But the ache lingered, as Janice had said, "a hole in their heart that is just Hannah size."

It was 2007. Ten years had passed since Hannah's death. Caleb and Josiah both played baseball and wrestled for their high school teams, while all the children, including Samuel, Gideon, and Abigail, kicked soccer balls with local teams through high school. Samuel and Gideon shone in their elementary years. The children's energy lit up the Camas fields, their new normal delicate yet flourishing, enlarged by their shared experiences of loss and love.

Gary's occasional calls to Waste Connections's owners, Ron Mittelstaedt and Darrell Chambliss, led to an unexpected invitation for dinner that included Caleb, now sixteen, and Josiah, thirteen. At the quiet dinner in the rustic Heathman Lodge in Vancouver, Ron and Darrell shared memories of her bright spirit, surprised by the growing family now numbering seven. Mari and Gary nodded, hands clasped, their ache still woven into a life reshaped by love and faith.

But they were there for a specific reason.

"We'd like to offer a scholarship to your boys," Ron told them.

This offer left them speechless, but after a few moments, Gary gulped and said, "We'd like to accept this offer. Of course, we'll send you the boys' grades to show you how they're doing."

"I would like that," Ron replied.

And so every semester, Ron received a copy of the boys' grades.

Life was better. College tuition was paid for two of their kids. Yet Hannah was still gone.

Front (left to right):
Gideon, Samuel, Abigail
Back: Caleb, Iosiah

The family at the top of Beacon Rock

Chapter 17

Growth Amid Trials

*Grieving is never anything we "get over." We're meant to live in it
and move through it, and out of that to live and be enlarged by that relationship
and those experiences. And yes, we create a new normal.*

~ Sandy

Around 2008, in the quiet evenings, though the children were thriving, the pain resurfaced, softer but unyielding. Mari and Gary, in the privacy of their bedroom, shared a glass of wine, the clink of glasses a fleeting comfort. Over time, the wine became a stronger cocktail, a nightly ritual to dull the vacuum of Hannah's absence. They always kept the alcohol in their bedroom, not within reach of their nearly adult children. The drinks became essential, a secret they hid behind their churchgoing smiles.

More than ten years passed. One morning, Mari opened her Bible to Psalm 90:8: "You spread out our sins before you—our secret sins—and you see them all" (NLT). The words struck her like a lightning bolt. Memories of her childhood flooded back—quiet abuse in the dark, secrets she was forbidden to share.

"Gary, we need to talk," she said that evening as he reached for the whiskey bottle. "I read this today. I hate secrets. I grew up with them, hiding what happened to me. This drinking—it's another secret. We can't keep doing this."

Gary paused, the bottle heavy in his hand. "Let me think about it," he said, his voice low.

The next day, driving his UPS route, the Columbia River glinting under a rare clear sky, he reflected. *The bottle numbs the pain, but it's still there when*

Abigail's high school graduation.
Left to right: Gideon, Samuel, Caleb, Abigail, Josiah

we wake. We can't handle this grief like this. The drinks felt flat that week, their comfort hollow.

"We need help, Mari," Gary said a few days later, setting the bottle aside. "What do we do?"

It was January 22, 2022, when the drinking stopped. Mari had searched the internet for help for Christians with an alcohol addiction. She found a group with a website. It said, "Alcoholics Victorious is a network of Christian support groups for chemically dependent persons. We believe that alcoholism is an addiction, and that the alcoholic is an individual who cannot, as a matter of will power alone, control his or her own dependency."[1]

Mari began attending this twelve-step program in Vancouver in October 2023, and Gary joined her when his work schedule permitted.

In their first meeting, the room warm with coffee and shared stories, a member named Sandy spoke softly. "Grief isn't something you get over," she said, her eyes kind. "You live through it, let it shape you, and build a new normal from it." Her words resonated, echoing Mari and Gary's journey through Hannah's loss.

---

1 "12 Steps of Alcoholics Anonymous," Alcoholics Victorious Headquarters, accessed September 23, 2025, https://www.alcoholicsvictorious.org/12-steps.

The family (left to right): Gideon, Abigail, Josiah, Caleb, Mari, Samuel, Gary

They learned others were also grappling with grief, abuse, or trauma.

"Most of us here are dealing with something," Sandy added. "You're not alone." Through this program, Mari and Gary found forgiveness and hope, their faith rekindled like at the Weekend to Remember years before.

Twenty-five years after Hannah died, Mari and Gary had overcome their reliance on alcohol, their evenings alive with the vibrancy of their growing family. Samuel and Gideon were in college. Abigail, a senior in high school, filled the house with song. She sounded a lot like Hannah.

Both Caleb and Josiah had played baseball and wrestled for their high school teams and now had graduated from college. But despite the family's new normal, Mari had a sense there might be something more.

"Gary, maybe there's one more thing we can do to help us," Mari said as they drove home from an Alcoholics Victorious meeting at the church.

"What's that?"

"I heard that a new GriefShare group is starting in January. Maybe we should go."

Chapter 18

Eternal Hope

He will wipe every tear from their eyes, and there will be no more death or sorrow or crying or pain. All these things are gone forever.
~ Revelation 21:4 NLT

In January 2024, Gary and Mari attended our GriefShare group[2] to make sure they had fully grieved their loss. That's where the beginnings of this book took place. Twenty-seven years later, they both acknowledge there is still pain. Yet they have hope.

Gary and Mari know they will see their little Hannah again one day. God took their pain of loss, like a patchwork quilt, where broken things are the tattered scraps—each tear and fray a story of wear. Scars are the bold, uneven stitches, not hiding the damage but binding it with strength. Every clumsy seam, every mended rip, weaves a tapestry that's flawed, yet unique. Proof that what's broken can still hold together, beautiful in its repair. But hope remains.

One Sunday, Mari confided to me she wanted to sing in the choir for the Christmas program held at church in December. "Do you think I could join?"

"I think you should," I said.

Mari's daughter, Abigail, told her that if she joined, she'd sing in the choir too. Between services at church, coffee and cookies are served. Gary and I happened to be sitting at the same table.

---

2 "Need Help Dealing with Grief?" GriefShare, accessed September 23, 2025, www. GriefShare.org.

He confided to me, "Mari told me she wondered why she was feeling sad the last couple of days." He shook his head, remembering their pain and loss. "Of course," he told her. "Don't you remember what day it is?"

It was December 15, one day before the twenty-seventh anniversary of Hannah's tragic accident.

That is what grief is: pain that captures thoughts of long ago. I watched Mari sing in the choir that Sunday, her face radiant amid the sanctuary's warm Christmas lights, contradicting the pain she carried. Despite the painful memories, Mari's joy-filled countenance shone as she sang, embodying Revelation 21:4: "He will wipe every tear from their eyes, and there will be no more death or sorrow or crying or pain. All these things are gone forever" (NLT).

Even though twenty-seven years had passed, the hearts of Mari and Gary still had a piece missing from the firstborn child they named Hannah Marguerite. Yet they anticipate the joy set before them.

They love their family and travel across the United States to visit their grandchildren.

At this writing, Samuel, their third son, and his wife Sarah have welcomed their second child, a girl. They named her Hannah.

Epilogue

Gary and Mari Malychewski, parents

Hannah, Caleb, Josiah, Samuel, Gideon, Abigail, children

Each of the children has a middle name that holds meaning for their parents, reflecting someone who influenced their lives:

- Elizabeth, for her paternal grandmother,
- Marguerite, for her maternal grandmother,
- Emil, for his paternal grandfather,
- Gary, for his father,
- Jonathon, for a pastor who discipled Gary and Mari early in their Christian walk, and
- Kyle, after Kyle Taylor, a boy who drowned in Texas.

Caleb is a physician's assistant and is training to become the administrator at a skilled nursing facility in Camas, Washington. He is married to Kylie and has a son.

Josiah has a degree in Communication from the University of Portland and is a recruiter for veterinarians across the United States.

Samuel lives in Eastern Oregon and serves in the National Guard. He has a degree in Molecular Biology from Eastern Oregon University. He is married to Sarah and has two daughters.

Gideon has a degree in Criminal Justice from Eastern Washington University and wishes to pursue employment in law enforcement. He lives in Camas.

Abigail has an AA degree from Clark College. She works part-time and lives in Camas.

Each child carries Hannah's spirit, their lives a testament to the family's resilience and faith.

Ron Mittelstaedt, CEO, and Darrell Chambliss, COO of Waste Connections, continue to lead the corporation from The Woodlands, Texas, Waste Connections Corporate Headquarters. Waste Connections is rapidly growing to an almost $10 billion company in 2025. Waste Connections Cares, their not-for-profit foundation, supports this book's publication. They maintain contact with Gary.

Kris Wright now manages a recycling and trash facility for Waste Connections in Canby, Oregon, and remains connected to the family's story.

Pastor Neal Curtiss serves on the support staff at Living Hope Church in Vancouver, Washington. He stays in touch with Gary and Mari, is married, and is the father of ten children and twenty-eight grandchildren.

Mari works part-time as a caregiver. She loves to travel with Gary, visiting their children and grandchildren. Mari's mother, Penny Marguerite, lives with the couple in Camas, Washington. Gary continues to drive for UPS.

Children play in the park near the home where they once lived, where a tree bears a plaque that says, "In honor of Hannah Marguerite Malychewski."

The angels that decorated the blue spruce tree all lit up for the family to see when they arrived home after Hannah's burial are still used every year to decorate their Christmas tree. Each year they add another angel to remember their Hannah.

On the hill at the end of "I" Street, above I-5, the blue spruce tree stands, growing tall and strong—a reminder of dear friends who cared for this family when they were hurting so badly.

Every December 16, the family gathers around a table laden with Chinese food, the aroma of sweet-and-sour sauce mingling with memories of Hannah's laughter. They remember that time so long ago when the family shared food and excitement after watching The Nutcracker. They share stories of her joy and hold fast to the hope that one day, all will be reunited. Through their journey of loss and faith, Hannah's enduring grace continues to guide them toward eternal hope.

It has been my honor to tell Gary and Mari's story. Their honesty and

recollections of their lives with me have reminded me of a precious passage in Isaiah 61:1–3:

> *The Spirit of the Sovereign LORD is on me,*
> *because the LORD has anointed me*
> *to proclaim good news to the poor.*
> *He has sent me to bind up the brokenhearted,*
> *to proclaim freedom for the captives*
> *and release from darkness for the prisoners,*
> *to proclaim the year of the LORD's favor*
> *and the day of vengeance of our God,*
> *to comfort all who mourn,*
> *and provide for those who grieve in Zion—*
> *to bestow on them a crown of beauty*
> *instead of ashes,*
> *the oil of joy*
> *instead of mourning,*
> *and a garment of praise*
> *instead of a spirit of despair.*
> *They will be called oaks of righteousness,*
> *a planting of the LORD*
> *for the display of his splendor.*

Acknowledgments

Writing Gary and Mari's story was a profound experience, more challenging than I anticipated when I began. Stepping into the grief and loss this couple endured was daunting, offering a glimpse of the immense pain Hannah's parents faced. I am deeply grateful to everyone who contributed to this book, bringing openness, insight, and support to this true story, now nearly twenty-eight years past.

To Gary and Mari, thank you for your courage in allowing me to explore your past and ask probing questions. Your transparency was invaluable, and I pray revisiting this tragedy fosters further healing.

My heartfelt thanks to those present on that fateful day—Ron Mittelstaedt, C.E.O. of Waste Connections, Darrell Chambliss, C.O.O. (retired), Kris Wright, Neal Curtiss, and others who shared their memories. Your recollections were essential in shaping a complete and authentic narrative. Finally, thank you to Waste Connections Cares for your support in publishing this book.

I am indebted to my editor, Rachel Bradley of Rachel's Revisions, whose tireless encouragement and insistence on precision refined my words and strengthened this story.

My gratitude to Kara of Mountain Creek Books for her artistry in designing the cover and guiding the publishing process with expertise.

To my writing groups, thank you for listening, offering suggestions, and praying with me throughout this journey. Your support was a lifeline.

To my beloved husband, Jim, thank you for your patience as I read, re-read, and discussed this book over many mornings. You are my rock and my star.

Above all, I give thanks to Jesus Christ, the Comforter who knows pain

more deeply than anyone. You walked with Gary and Mari through their loss and with me in writing and rewriting this story. You have been my strength through my own pain and loss, and I am forever grateful to You, my Rock and Redeemer.

About the Authors

Shirley Quiring Mozena is a retreat leader and a national speaker for Stonecroft Ministries. Her website, shirleymozena.com, features blogs, her speaking schedule, and options to purchase her books, including other titles. Shirley has authored five books centered on hope and encouragement amid life's challenges, with a deep passion for guiding those grieving the loss of loved ones toward healing. Alongside her husband, Jim, she facilitates GriefShare at their church. They live in Southwest Washington State.

Shirley cherishes her large blended family, delights in entertaining at home, and enjoys walking her lively Yorkie-mix, Rudy.

Gary and Mari Malychewski live in the country outside of Camas, Washington. They love their growing family, and enjoy traveling to see them. Gary drives for UPS, and Mari is a caregiver.

Other Books by Shirley

Second Chance at Love:
A Practical Guide to Remarriage after Loss

Whether your marriage was blissful or challenging, lengthy or short, it didn't end the way you imagined. Regardless of how you found yourself without a life partner, you may be at a point where you'd like to experience the love of a spouse again. Authors Shirley and Jim Mozena experienced devastating losses and then struggles in their relationships before finding renewed love with each other, and in Second Chance at Love they offer their insights to these difficult questions:

- Are you really ready?
- Is now the time?
- How do you know if you've found the right one?
- Is the potential pain of losing another spouse worth it?

The authors approach their answers with practical reality and their own vulnerability. They share the experiences of their first marriages, their second marriages, their journeys through what seemed like devastating losses, and the gifts of finding love and another chance to share their lives with a spouse after death and divorce.

In addition to the down-to-earth guidance on the situations you face when considering marrying again, Shirley and Jim have created valuable questionnaires to identify issues and facilitate discussions with potential mates. The information contained in this book will give you confidence and peace as you navigate these hopeful waters.

Second Chance at Love: A Practical Guide to Remarriage after Loss
is available at Shirley's website (shirleymozena.com)
or on amazon.com and barnesandnoble.com

Second Chances at Life and Love, with Hope

When Shirley and Bill set out on a dream trip in the beautiful northwest wilderness to celebrate their 40th anniversary, what develops is a nightmare that has no end. Mysterious pangs turn into a vicious virus that makes its way into Bill's body. Shirley finds comfort through her Savior during the six months of Bill's illness—an illness which eventually takes his life.

After a time, Shirley's heart aches for companionship. Little does she know that living a few miles from her home, a widower mourns the loss of his wife of 32 years. They meet and fall hopelessly in love, and their love takes them on a two-year journey of joy and adventure until once again overwhelming heartbreak rocks Shirley's world. This is a story of faith and courtship to strengthen your own soul.

Praise for *Second Chances*:

This story is wonderfully written with honesty and the depth of understanding that only grief can bring. In spite of the sad story of loss, the message of the book is one of joy in the goodness of today and hope for a future with God.

—**Jan Pierce**, author

Be ready for an "all-nighter" once you open this book. Shirley shares her times of love, sorrow, joy, peace and renewal. Shirley's willingness to open her heart to help others is seen throughout the book.

—**Judi Mayfield**, author

I just finished reading Second Chances. *Thank you for sharing your story with authenticity and candor... your trust in our kind Father has been your bedrock...*

—**Diane Stevens**

Second Chances **is available at Shirley's website (shirleymozena.com) or on amazon.com and barnesandnoble.com**

Beyond Second Chances

The true story of a woman, twice widowed, who finds fulfilling love again. After grappling with loneliness, Shirley enters a hasty courtship, and is crushed by a broken engagement just before the wedding. Once again, Shirley's dreams have been destroyed. In her grief, she fully surrenders to God, faces her challenges and learns to trust Him more deeply.

Praise for *Beyond Second Chances*:
I just finished your book and wish so much that I had read it BEFORE meeting you and Jim in Branson at Hope Restored. You are both living proof that our generous God does restore hope, because He loves us so personally.

—**Rona**, Colorado Springs, CO

Beyond Second Chances **is available at Shirley's website (shirleymozena.com) or on amazon.com and barnesandnoble.com**

Trustworthy Anchor

God promises to be a trustworthy anchor in the calm moments as well as in the storms that come to your life. The meditations, coupled with the author's inspirational stories, will inspire you to find hope, encouragement, and joy.

"We began a new intimacy with each other, not just the oneness of sexual intimacy but heart intimacy. We felt freer to share our inner thoughts with each other. I began to trust, revealing my true feelings…"

"God cares about every detail of our lives, including resentment we might be carrying from long ago. It isn't healthy, and it hurts us, not the other person."

"Looking back over my life, I've learned in the difficult moments and scary times that if I went to God for refuge and safety…I felt the safety of his protection. There were still troubles, but when I ran to him, I felt secure. I knew I wasn't alone."

When the storm comes, you'll be fully anchored and grounded in the Savior's love. That's when the anchor digs deeper and keeps you steady.

Trustworthy Anchor is available at Shirley's website (shirleymozena.com) or on amazon.com and barnesandnoble.com

I love reading non-fiction. There is power and meaning in reading true stories to which everyone can relate. Shirley does a masterful job of telling the story of a family's struggle in her book, Remembering Hannah: A Journey Through Loss with Hope. As a high school counselor, I helped many students deal with the grief of loss. As the parent of six adopted children, my wife and I dealt with many ups and downs in our family. Shirley's book is a good resource to help us understand the feelings of grief, how difficult it is to work through, and how the loss of a child can affect so many people. This book is a powerful story that will touch anyone's emotions, while giving help in dealing with grief and providing encouragement and hope. I can heartily recommend Remembering Hannah for all parents to read and anyone who has been touched by the loss of a family member or friend's child.

Jim McConnell
Retired Teacher, School Counselor
Camas, Washington

Shirley Mozena has brought her exceptional talents to write a compelling true story of hope, love, forgiveness, and personal redemption in the face of heartbreaking tragedy and loss. It reveals the power of faith and the grace of God when it was needed most. I believe this story will bless all who read it and bring a measure of healing for many who have walked down a similar road.

Rich Blum
Senior Pastor, Bethel Community Church
Washougal, Washington

There are life memories that never fade. Experiences that are etched in our minds and hearts that seem as though they happened yesterday. Hannah is one of those memories. In Remembering Hannah: A Journey Through Loss with Hope, Shirley Quiring Mozena brings to life the vibrant joy of a little girl, the warm family she lived with, and the tragic accident that changed people's lives forever. Life is hard, and sometimes things happen that don't make sense, that leave us with more questions than answers, and Hannah's short-lived life was like that. Shirley writes with compassion, understanding, and wonderful insight, as she tells the story of Hannah, the challenges that Gary and Mari went through following her death, and how their faith became their stronghold even as they struggled to cope with the loss of their daughter. This story will grip your heart and take you on a journey that will change you. If you have suffered loss, you will find hope in these pages as Shirley describes how this little girl's life still impacts people today. Thank you Gary and Mari for allowing us to share in your deepest heartache and pain, and thank you Shirley for bringing us back to the hope we have in Jesus and for helping us remember this special girl named Hannah!

Neal Curtiss
Pastor, Living Hope Church
Vancouver, Washington

Remembering Hannah